Copyright © 2020 by Mike Artell
All rights reserved. Neither this book nor any portion thereof may be reproduced or used in any manner whatsoever without the express written permission of the publisher except for brief excerpts for classroom use.

Printed in the United States of America

ISBN 9781732418042

MJA Creative, LLC
P.O. Box 3997
Covington, LA 70434
www.mikeartell.com

My Shetland pony plays guitar,
I know that's strange of course.
But he's not just a pony, dude,
He's like... a rockin' horse.

Chimpanzees will use their feet
To peel and eat bananas.
But don't do that, or else we'll think
That you ain't got no mannas.

Potbelly pigs are big bags of jelly
Potbelly pigs are chubby and short.
Potbelly pigs are clean, they're not smelly
And when they are happy, they snort.

Potbelly pigs are cute when they're little
Potbelly pigs are fun when they're small.
But Potbelly pigs get big in the middle
And soon they can't walk down the hall.

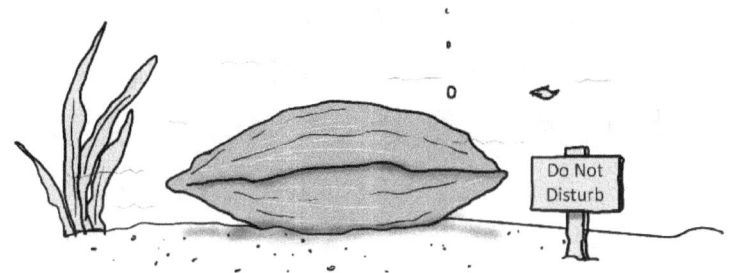

Oysters are the perfect pet
All you do is keep them wet.
Tell them "sit" and tell them "stay"
And they never disobey.

If something happened to my
cute,
fuzzy,
cuddly,
squeaky,
little gerbil,
That would be terbil.

Oh my gosh! My dog has fleas!
In his ears and on his knees!
Puppy starts to whine and grrrr
As the fleas crawl in his fur.
Then he starts to bite and scratch,
(Fleas are small and hard to catch).

O.K. fleas, we've had enough,
You have forced me to get tough.
I'll buy flea soap, powder too,
And some anti-flea shampoo.

Adios, fleas! Sayonara!
Hope I don't see you tomorra.

Looking for a pet?
A skunk would fit you well
If you don't have any friends
Who have a sense of smell.

Weenie dog is long and low
With ears that drag the ground.
On the front she's kinda pointy
On the back, she's round.

Weenie dog will bark real loud
To make sure that we heard her.
There is no dog cuter than
My lovable frankfurter.

My hamster runs in circles inside his little wheel
He isn't going anywhere, but that is no big deal.
Hampsters don't need destinations
When they start to run,
They don't run to go somewhere,
Hampsters run for fun.

When my cockatoo is blue
I tickle my pet cockatoo.
And when my cocker spaniel's blue
I tickle my pet cocker too.

I should get a badge for merit
Since I own a smelly ferret.
Ferrets have a non-stop motor
And a most unpleasant odor.
And they all have A.D.D.
Gee...
Ferrets are a lot like ME!

Pretty little kitty cat, you're a powder puff
But you shed your kitty hair
all over all our stuff.
Silky hair like yours is nice,
I just wish you would keep it.
When you shed it then I have to
Pick it up or sweep it.

I like my dog. I like my cat.
I don't know which is better.
My dog will come each time I call,
My cat? I have to go and get her.

Two iguana poems

It's neater to eat a tortilla
But it's sweeter to eat a fajita.
Tomorrow (In Spanish: mañana),
I'm planning to eat an iguana.

I want a pet iguana
Today and not mañana.
I asked my mother, "por favor"
She just said, "no" and nothing more.

Three dog poems

Pilgrims didn't want dogs yapping
When they were below deck napping.
No one had a pet Chihuahua
On the Pilgrim ship Mayflhuahua.

English sheepdogs' eyes
are covered
by their hairy tresses,
So they find out
where they are
by using GPSes.

If you're walking down the street
and your dog makes poop,
Please don't leave it laying there
stoop and scoop the goop.

One long cat poem

There is nothing that is cuter
Than my cat at her computer.
She sends Tweets and emails too
To her friends in CATmandu.
Sometimes she will start a chat
With a Himalayan cat,
And then other social kitties
Join the chat from different cities.
Soon the cat room chatroom grows
Filled with Manx and Calicos.
Then a Bengal, Bombay too
Join the Rex and Russian Blue.
It's a worldwide kitty chat
Started by my kitty cat.
All across the Internet
Kitties chat with friends they've met.
When they're done they say, "Meow"
Cats know that means, "Bye for now!"

Little baby alligator
You are very sweet
With your little gator tail
And your gator feet.

One day you'll be big and strong
Like your gator mother
And with any luck at all
You will eat my brother.

(Author's note: Just kidding about eating your brother.)

The dinostore is where you go
To buy a dino pet.
The dinostore has dino-groomers
And a dino-vet.
The dinostore has dino-houses
And some dino-lights,
And if you like explosions,
you can buy some dino-mites.

Me: Mom, can I have a pet?
Mom: You bet!
Me: Can I have a horse?
Mom: Of course!
Me: Can I keep it in my room?
Mom: I assume.
Me: Can it wear dad's clothes?
Mom: I suppose.
Me: You're kidding I suspect.
Mom: You're correct.

Some dogs shed,
Some dogs don't.
Some dogs' fur falls,
Some dogs' won't.

Here are dogs
That do not shed,
They can sleep
With you in bed:
Bichon Frise,
Giant Schnauzer
Irish Water Spaniel.
Taking care of them is easy
You won't need a manual.
Some dogs shed,
But these will not.
That's why I like them all a lot.

I know a small boy they call Chucky
Who lives on a farm in Kentucky
His pet isn't real
But that's no big deal
He's happy with his rubber ducky.

Hermit crabs won't share their homes,
It's not that they are selfish
There's just no room inside that shell
To squeeze another shellfish.

Tarantula, tarantula
Inside your habitat
Scaring people with your fangs
Yo dude, what is up with that?

Tarantula, tarantula,
I'll give you some advice, sir:
Lose the fangs and all the hair
And you would look much nicer.

My Labrador retriever
Loves to fetch a tennis ball.
She's played this game with me
Since she's been very small.

She never seems to want to stop
It's what she likes the best,
Back and forth and back and forth,
She never stops to rest.

Eventually, we have to quit
Although this game is cool.
Because the ball gets soaked
With Labrador retriever drool.

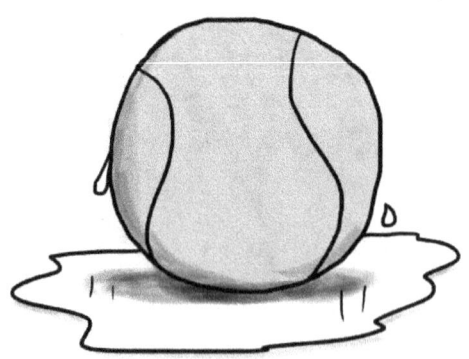

When I have to take my fish somewhere
I leave them in their aquarium.
I find that doing that is better
Than trying to catch and carium.

I do not like the petting zoo,
I always come home scarred.
That's because the tigers
Always pet me
W-a-a-a-y too hard.

A fly flew in my right ear
And out the other side.
I guess there wasn't anything
With which it could collide.

Porcupines are very prickly.
So when they hug,
They must hug
Quickly.

Two disturbing bug poems

I lifted up a rock and found
A little bug upon the ground.
How would it taste? I was suspicious,
So gulp, chew, ahhh... it was delicious!

I have two disturbing news flashes:
First, bugs live on your eyelashes.
Disturbing news flash number two:
They eat the dead skin off of you.

(Author's note: It's true. There really are little critters living on your eyelashes.)

My chameleon is gone
Or maybe it's not.
Chameleons are tricky
They're real hard to spot.
Chameleons change color
To match what they're on
They do it so well
They look like they're gone.
Would it be wrong and
Would it be bad
To put my chameleon
On something that's plaid?

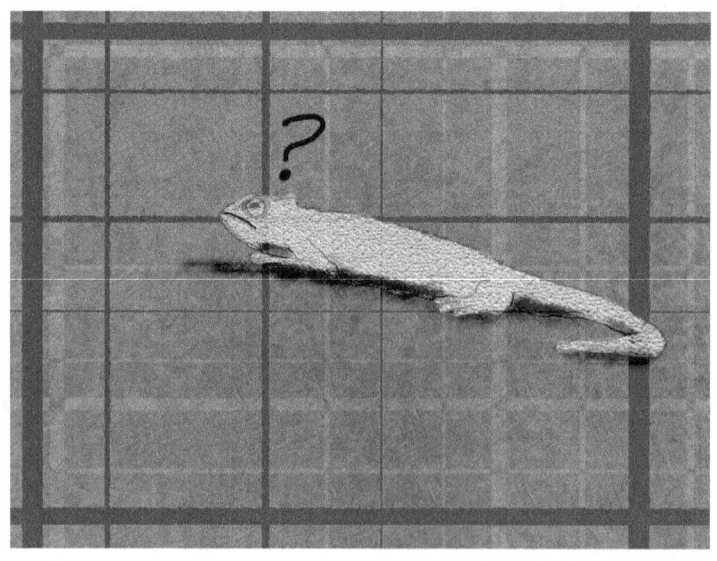

In the Arctic where it's cold
Polar bears are very bold.
They hang out on their icy floats
All toasty warm in big fur coats.

Little mouse, you are so cute
In your furry mousey suit.
Little whiskers on your nose,
Little toenails on your toes.
But your sniffing never ceases,
Could the cause be mousey sneezes?

Little Miss Muffet sat on a tuffet
Eating her curds and whey.
Along came a spider and sat down beside her
And frightened Miss Mufett away.

Miss Muffet came back with a can in a sack,
It was bug spray she bought at the store.
The spider's now gone
from Miss Muffet's lawn
And it sure won't be back anymore.

Do sheepdogs baa or do they bark
When they call their sheepdog pup?
Do sheepdogs baa or do they bark?
And do they ever get mixed up?

**A Short, Sad Poem
About A Frog
Who Didn't Pay Attention
While Crossing The Road
And Ended Up
Being Hit By A Car**

Hop, hop, hop.

BOP!

Plop.

I like insects, I like bugs
They're my pets I give them hugs.
Bring them candy and corsages
Give them neck and back massages.
Read them books and magazines
Dress them up in baggy jeans.
Pat them on their little heads
Tuck them into buggy beds.
Six legs, eight legs, even more
Crawling on my bedroom floor.
Bugs are very cool to me
I love entomology.

Though Little Bo Peep has lost a sheep
She doesn't really mind it.
The sheep is alone,
But it has a cell phone
So Bo knows where to find it.

Another Little Bo Peep poem

Little Bo Pip has lost her ship.
Uh...I mean...
Little Bo Pup has lost her cup.
No...um..lemme see...
Little Bo Poop has lost her group.
Aw, forget it. I'd rather take a nap
Than say any more about Little Bo Pap.

The Funny Farm

(Author's note: Add your own music to this
poem and sing it or add a beat
and do it as a rap.)

Let's skedaddle arm-in-arm,
Ride down to the Funny Farm.
Brush your teeth and comb your hair,
Take a bus we'll soon be there!
Doodle bugs and big galoots
Wear tall hats and cowboy boots.
Early birds and sitting ducks
Drive around in pickup trucks.
Chubby piggies sing off-key,
Tra-la-la and do-re-mi.
Cows bounce on the trampoline
While the mice get squeaky clean.
Cockamamie roosters crow
At the buffed-up buffalo.

With their tootsies in the sink,
Rabbits' feet get tickled pink.
Horses wearing monkey suits
Guzzle all the tutti-fruits.
Gooney birds play peek-a-boo,
Sweet patooties boogaloo.
Lovebirds with their goo-goo eyes
Sing their babies lullabies.
Hootenanny goats high-five,
Skunks learn how to scuba dive.
Hee-haw donkey brays and snorts,
Runs around in boxer shorts.
It starts raining cats and dogs,
Frightens fifteen freckled frogs.
Catch you later! Gotta run!
Funny Farm was so much fun!

Mike Artell has written dozens and dozens of books, most of which he also illustrated.

You can find out more about Mike's books, videos, and school visits on his web site: www.mikeartell.com

www.ingramcontent.com/pod-product-compliance
Lightning Source LLC
Chambersburg PA
CBHW070120110526
44587CB00016BA/2737